Live wit
Reckless A
Much Love
Shateke

RECKLESS
ABANDONMENT

Becoming Free for God's Purpose

By Shateka Husser

DEDICATION

I dedicate this book to my mother, father, siblings, nieces, nephew, 7 God children, family and friends.

ACKNOWLEDGEMENTS

I would like to give acknowledgement to Jesus Christ, my Lord and Savior, the late Angie Thornewell who became my book finishing accountability partner without being asked, as well as my friend Tammi Nichols who passionately helped with pre-edits.

PREFACE

Sometimes, our calling can seem overwhelming and even shocking. In fact, there have been times when I've found myself talking in front of a group of people only to remember that I'm not really a "talking in front of people" kind of person. But, as I have led in both spiritual and nonspiritual environments, I'm experiencing God—his mind and wisdom—stretching and working within me.

This last year has been a year of great reflection. It has been a year of great loss and great joy, and I have developed a sense of urgency because of it—an urgency to set boundaries like never before so that I can stay right in the face of God, to move away from my desires, as great as they may be, to pursue only the purpose God has been calling me to. In doing that, I'm taking on a new form of "reckless abandonment." Let me tell you, God has made some abrupt changes in my life. Yet, as I suddenly left the corporate world, I found that God showed up in a mighty way to provide for all the needs that I had as I pursued and prioritized his vision for my life instead of my own desire and plan.

It hasn't always been that way in my life. Like everyone else, I have lived my life according to my own understanding and vision, pursuing what most of us do, society's definition of success. However, I have learned that the plans God has for our purpose matter most. This book is the first product God has called me to do.

INTRODUCTION

Have you ever said to yourself, "There's got to be more to life than this!" not because you didn't have a blessed life or were unsuccessful, but because you knew there had to be more meaning and purpose than the daily routines of your life. You knew there had to be a greater sense of purpose and deeper meaning. You knew you were created to experience more and be more, but what and who? Perhaps you were a public success but felt like a private failure in the areas of fulfillment and contentment. Perhaps there was a void you couldn't quite put your finger on or understand because you already had the career, the love of family and friends, the business, the fame, and a luxurious lifestyle, but there was still something missing.

May I invite you to go on a quick journey of understanding about what that missing part just might be?

If you're a believer, you've said the model prayer mentioned in Mathew 6:9-13:

After this manner therefore pray ye: Our Father which art in heaven, Hallowed be thy name. Thy kingdom come. Thy will be done in earth, as it is in heaven. Give us this day our daily bread. And forgive us our debts, as we forgive our debtors. And lead us not into temptation, but deliver us from evil: For thine is the kingdom, and the power, and the glory, forever. Amen.

You've prayed, "Thy will be done in earth, as it is in heaven....", and then you hopped up after the prayer and continued on with your life's journey. You may have even given a little more thought to his will but taken no real action to execute it. Well, at some point, we have to get to a place where we totally surrender to God's will, purpose, and plan for our lives. At some point, we must recklessly abandon our vision for His. Who is he? Jesus, the Holy Spirit, who lives in his human creations, us. He never leaves or forsakes us.

In II Chronicles 16:9, he says he's looking for people whom he can make strong, but it requires our hearts to be totally committed to

Him. The Holy Spirit desires to move within us without restriction in guiding us along this short life's journey. Jesus wants to greatly manifest himself in the actions of people. He wants to live vicariously through us so our lives are impacted in the most incredible way. Full-time ministry is the mandate of every believer to be an ambassador of the faith, which is not confined to the four corners of a church; rather, it's in our every response, interaction, and relationship with other believers and nonbelievers in the most loving way. Some of us have been called to operate in church roles (priestly anointing) where we're most effective; others are called to operate in marketplace roles (kingly anointing) where we are most effective; and there's a few who are stretched to operate in both realms.

The scriptures remind us repeatedly how God is jealous and that he wants to be first in our lives. When we chase after everything but Him, He will send the wrath of disruption to those he decides to chasten. Notice I said, "to those he decides," because they are chosen based on his design for their lives and not on their own designs.

We were all bought with a price, but unlike slavery, we were bought to be *free*. *Freedom* is required in order for each of us to live life more abundantly. Most of all, that *freedom* is necessary so we can maneuver most effectively on his behalf. Other fruits, manifesting from *freedom*, include but is not limited to the favor and wisdom of God and greater impact, influence, and income for stewardship over the Kingdom's business.

Only a privileged few who are chosen to fully surrender their will to his, and as a result, are exceptional stewards of God's glory and will experience the triple effects of increased impact, influence, and income.

With wisdom, He consistently gives these Kingdom tools to those he trusts.

Today, I'm very excited to be living my recklessly abandoned life before God and to see how he shows up each and every day as I teach and lead the people he has assigned to me. After working as a corporate leader, and before that serving as a military leader, nothing beats having Abba Father, Jesus, as my marketplace boss. My life has been forever disrupted. It's in him I'm most capable of making boss moves. It's in him I have moved from success to successful significance, and it's in him I have my very being. Now, I have the opportunity to take the experiences that God has given me coupled with the word planted in me to influence career and business professionals to take strategic action in their own lives. I want you to know that I believe in you; but more importantly, you can believe in yourself and know that you were created to be and live in this world authentically and in harmony to his greater directing.

We all have the same opportunity to move forward, not with a lot of self-thoughts, not with our plans, but with the weight of the calling within us and the urgency to do what we were placed on this earth to do—pursuing God's will instead of our desires. By living in what I call "reckless abandonment," we're empowered to thrive in bold, radical, and obedient action. I know firsthand how uncomfortable and inconvenient this seems, but it is necessary for both personal growth and advancement in God's Kingdom.

When you're stretched from where you are to where you're going, it might feel like a demonic attack when it's really spiritual birthing pains.

You're pregnant with purpose that's causing you to soar higher than the vision you have for yourself. You have to think bigger and imagine more because God has a plan so much greater than our limited imagination. He's the same God of companies like Apple, Facebook, Walmart, Amazon, and so many more. They were all birthed from an incredible vision God created.

I get it; thinking, living this way is extremely uncomfortable with many unknowns, especially when you've always felt somewhat in control of your life, albeit with false securities of a job or career that were never meant to be your ultimate source. The Lord allows various negative circumstances to affect us so we become uncomfortable enough to make the decision to change, take the leap of faith, and surrender our will for his.

His ultimate desire is for us to partner with him, pursue and prioritize his purpose over our plan, and to perform and produce at our greatest potential. So, ultimately, he receives his return on investment out of our creation.

Every day really is a gift, and when we look

at it that way, we ask ourselves questions like, "How can I repay God for allowing me one more day of grace?" While in the past I sporadically thought about this, it's becoming more of a habit ever since I suddenly lost my two closest friends in the first week of March 2018. Death allows us to take inventory of our existence, not for our glory, but for God's glory.

It's our responsibility to see that God gets his ROI (return on investment) from our lives before we transition.

He said, "Greater works shall you do." But he knew it would require his power, so he left his Holy Spirit to do just that. It's up to us whether we choose to use it for empowerment or take it for granted, never tapping into our greater selves. A life coach, pastor, therapist, friend, or spouse can never empower us the way the Holy Spirit can. They can never tell us our purpose or help us realize our identity. This can only be found in Christ Jesus. While it might take decades or a lifetime, it's imperative we find our authentic identity, know our divine purpose, and prioritize them over our many unimportant, trivial, yet busy activities.

TABLE OF CONTENTS

SECTION I

DIVORCE BONDAGES

"Bondages are distractions to his will and purpose for your life."

Shateka Husser

CHAPTER 1

Reckless Abandonment And Freedom

"Stand fast therefore in the liberty wherewith Christ hath made us *free*, and be not entangled again with the yoke of bondage." Galations 5: 1

"Reckless abandonment," simply put, is a mind-set. The term reckless means to do something without thought or thought of consequence. So, to "recklessly abandon" something is to think, "no matter what it is, no matter what the consequences may be, or how it's going to turn out, I've decided to take radical action and to prepare myself for a greater purpose and goal."

Although previously cherished—your life might have been super amazing—the preparation or time for change is imminent, if not immediate. The reason for this change is usually about a personal *freedom*, goal, or something of greater importance.

To abandon something you once cherished and decide to move forward in a different direction in hopes of a more fruitful life can be extremely disruptive to your norm. It might be inconvenient and uncomfortable. However, your search for greater *obedience* to God, greater relationships, greater income, greater impact, greater influence, greater peace, or whatever your "greater" is will force you to finally take radical action.

So, most people think twice or ponder long, but when you recklessly abandon something or someone, you make a "no-matter-what" decision. It's a decision to move forward without thinking about it anymore because it is for a greater good. It's about being really decisive and taking steps of no return. Many times, our stagnation is linked to something we know we need to stop (or start, or both stop and start), but we procrastinate for whatever reason, and there's so many different reasons, right? They may include fearing consequences, not being clear on strategy, needing more time or information, perfectionism, competing priorities, needing more information, not feeling capable, thinking the worse, and so much more.

The movie *Widows* is a clear example of this "no matter what" decision making. The *widows* had nothing to lose and everything to gain if they could just follow through with a rigorous, detailed, and flawlessly executed plan. Their husbands did not leave any of them a financial inheritance. They were all in poverty after losing their husbands and this strategic plan was critical to their financial future and well-being. There was no room for thinking negatively, although the reality is that things could have gone sideways. As in that movie and in our lives, we have to realize and understand that unless we take action, unless we move to the very next step, we will never know the endless possibilities that await us. So, Ephesians 3:20 tells us that the reality of what God can accomplish exceeds our wildest expectations and imagination. In other words, even if you could imagine it, the reality could be so much more. This process of imagining what you want is called *visualization* and is an exercise many coaches. This process allows clients the opportunity to visualize their ideal life vision. Take a quick moment to visualize what you believe God is saying concerning your life before you continue reading. Many times God-sized visions seem impossible but we have to exercise greater faith.

When you get that winning mindset—believing in yourself—you will always take action. The act of abandonment may just be the action you need to aggressively move forward. Abandonment is a by-product of your passion for next.

Faith unlocks the door but wise action is the key.

According to Matthew 22:14: "Many are called but few are chosen." For those of you who know you're chosen to do more for the Kingdom, you may have to forfeit your life plan for God's will. This "reckless abandonment" is necessary. He challenges each and every one of us to grow in his image. The bondage and glass ceiling many of the chosen experience is a result of dis*obedience* and the resulting curses they bring upon their own lives. They're bound by poor decisions made from selfishness rather than surrendering. For those of you who say you aren't chosen, you're still called, and you still have a part to play in promoting the message of Christ through your daily living.

Don't be a person who binds yourself to mediocrity and experiences unnecessary obstacles to realizing your best life as a result of not having *freedom*. When it comes to your true identity, God's purpose is revealed. When you prioritize your ideal life plan over his purpose for creating you, you open yourself up to self-sabotage, bondage, and unfruitfulness. He was clear when he told us to be fruitful (our most productive selves) and multiply. With our productivity comes multiplication and we reap more than the harvest we sow. Whenever we are confused and our progress and momentum stagnate, it is because of a misalignment of his will with our will. As he said in Romans 8:28, "All things work together for the good of them who are called according to his (not their) purpose."

Freedom: What Does It Mean to Be *Free*?

There's a surface *freedom* and then there's a deeper *freedom*. Surface *freedom* means just that, the obvious. However, deeper *freedom* has to be evaluated with careful thought. It's revealed through a sense of greater self-awareness and an intentional pursuit of understanding how you're spiritually aligned. This deeper *freedom* affects your soul, emotions, and will. For example, when you're bound by money (the spirit of mammon-Luke 16:13KJV), it's possible you're a slave to debt and will base most of your decisions on having to pay bills or sustaining a standard of living higher than you can afford. Additionally, the more you earn, the more dissatisfied you become and seek to earn even more out of greed and not need. Matthew 6:24 NIV says,

"No one can serve two masters. Either you will hate the one and love the other, or you will be devoted to the one and despise the other. You cannot serve both God and money."

Your freedom ideally flows from his purpose because his way is easy and his burden is light.

Even when you're bound to others, you're *free* in him because of the peace you experience. This peace comes from living your most authentic life without compromise, restraint, regret, shame, or bondage.

The sooner people realize they're bound, how they became bound, and have a desire to be *free*, the sooner they move into real action toward a more abundant life. They take full responsibility, own it, and commit to change, transformation, or reinvention of their lives. It's like being in an unhealthy relationship you no longer want to be in: You find a way to become *free* again. You *free* yourself from the commitment, any previous obligations, and you effectively communicate your decision so there's no false sense of commitment.

To live restricted in any way, whether from self-imposed or external reasons, is to live in a way that is inauthentic. Living this way is the reason behind many bad decisions, why so many people never get married, get divorced, never go into the military, never get saved, never have children, never establish new friendships, and so many other negative behaviors.

There are several definitions of what it means to be *free*, and it really depends on the individual and what season of life he or she is in. A few definitions are the following:

1. Not being under the control or power of another; able to act as one wishes

2. Not physically restrained, obstructed, or fixed; unimpeded

3. Not subject to or constrained by engagements or obligations; unoccupied, available, not busy or overcommitted

4. Not subject to or affected by a specified thing, typically an undesirable one

5. Being frank or unrestrained in speech, expression, or action; not acting in any way to please people

I will touch on some aspect of each of these definitions throughout this section. There's nothing worse than being restricted although there are times when it could be beneficial, for example, until a person reaches greater levels of maturity. An even worse situation is to become *free* and then find yourself tied and tangled up with a person who is still bound and trying to help *free* that individual all the while knowing you aren't the savior nor were you created to *free* others.

What does it mean to be *free*? This book explores levels of bondage many people struggle to gain *freedom* from.

One thing to ponder and embrace are those bondages prohibiting you from soaring higher in purpose. True *freedom* requires divorcing them. Beyond restrictions of *freedom*, there are usually two things preventing people from accomplishing this. The first is trouble submitting to God's will because of having personal desires, and the second is lacking the capacity to execute, with consistency, actions of skill and wisdom.

The next few chapters should help you discover some of the roadblocks preventing you from moving forward in God's purpose.

Once you break *free*, soaring higher will be seamless if your desires and capacity are aligned. Consistency of actions will become a nonissue. Your passion will be restored. Your strategy will be revised. You will break *free* and break through to higher heights with greater impact on the world!

CHAPTER 2

Break *Free* from Heart Conditions

"Hope deferred maketh the heart sick: but when the desire cometh, it is a tree of life." Proverbs 13:12

This entire book really is about our "heart posture." Of course this posture has nothing to do with the physical condition of your heart; instead, the primary condition of the attitude you're harboring in your soul (mind, will, and emotions). In order to recklessly abandon our will for his, we must examine our heart and determine what's not congruent with his will. On the surface, before we discover deeper layers during our intimate times of worship, the heart could be deceiving us into believing it is entirely healthy.

The heart houses our desires, and if those desires are misaligned with God's will, this could not only cause heartache but also rob us of living in the present and enjoying life.

This misalignment could be centered on the wrong person, career, business, dream, goal, and so on.

Whenever I think of hope, I think of the phrase, "having only positive expectations." I know many of you have heard this saying, and I think it's the perfect statement describing hope. Hope says everything will now be all right. When hope is not present, despondency, or depression, sets in. That depression prevents us from moving forward, binding us to the fears of hopelessness. I now understand that my hope was built more on the carnal (temporary) than the spiritual (infinity). So my mood was often affected by temporary, seasonal circumstances. My hope was saturated in false identity, often defined by roles (church, military, and corporate) rather than on who Jesus meant me to be. I was consumed with all sorts of role busyness and wrong priorities.

Here's two examples of a heart posture:

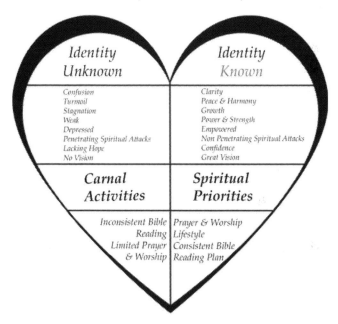

Identity Unknown	*Identity Known*
Confusion	Clarity
Turmoil	Peace & Harmony
Stagnation	Growth
Weak	Power & Strength
Depressed	Empowered
Penetrating Spiritual Attacks	Non Penetrating Spiritual Attacks
Lacking Hope	Confidence
No Vision	Great Vision
Carnal Activities	**Spiritual Priorities**
Inconsistent Bible Reading	Prayer & Worship Lifestyle
Limited Prayer & Worship	Consistent Bible Reading Plan

Without hope, we experience so many negative emotions that include not only discouragement but also primarily fear, then disappointment, and finally frustration. Proverbs 13:12 says "Hope deferred maketh the heart sick: but when the desire cometh, it is a tree of life." When the heart becomes sick and contaminated with issues, void of hope, it can manifest physically as heartache along with erratic behavior, abrasive interactions, and vulgar communication.

Additionally, strong surges of uncontrollable emotions can cause panic attacks. This may evolve from the experience of pain laced with rejection, abandonment, change, disappointment, loss of a loved one, and so much more. However, once your mind shifts to a powerfully positive state of mind, your heart will become *free*. Out of this abundance of your heart, your mind speaks to you. To have hope is to have great faith instead of great fear. Until people can shift their minds, they'll never shift their lives. But when they finally do shift their minds, they'll shift their lives with more positive responses, communication, behaviors, and life-altering decision making.

That's why it's important to "keep hope alive," as the saying goes, by having an effective source of "hope nutrition." I can only point you to one source: Jesus. When you find a person with great hope, you'll find a person in the right relationship with Jesus. Jesus is our help and our hope. He causes us to believe in the impossible and imagine the possibilities. With him, we know all things are possible. In him, we can do all things and should expect the new. His omniscience is beyond our limited beliefs and thoughts, so it's never wise to put him in a box. Instead of being someone who is faithless and powerless in the face of great adversity, I challenge you to think differently and experience a paradigm shift of hope.

If we could see some of our desires as negative, it would *free* us faster; we would become *free* of false expectations. What if, for example, we are hoping for the wrong things? What if what we want doesn't align with God's will for our life? Could what we hope for be wrong? Is the passion we hope for ironically not our real purpose? Could we be hoping for success but with our success ladder leaning up against the wrong wall?

We should have hope but we should also be careful not to hope in error. When we hope in error, we rob our lives of the present joys God desires for our extraordinary lives.

Growing up, I knew a lady who was a believer. She became saved while she was married, but then her husband left her. Imagine that. For as long as I can remember, all my life and into my adult years, she was steadfast in her belief that her husband was coming back. She even went as far as to say God told her he was sending him back. I'm sad to report that she has since passed on to glory and her husband never came back. She hoped in error as so many of us have done. We become bound to a false hope, aborting God's better plan and missing out on many fruitful years of contentment and happiness.

We've all experienced times of feeling empty, a void. These feelings often manifest in mild to severe depression. Sometimes, we feel this way because we are unable to fulfill a desire and become so oppressed by what we don't have rather than being grateful for what we do. This oppression doesn't come from being a slave, being in prison, or being controlled by any external event or person; it comes from within our own heart.

Sometimes, what's in our heart is the very thing in conflict with God's will for us, and as a result, we never experience his supernatural peace.

Unloving Interactions

The heart impacts our interactions and relationships. It controls what's verbally communicated because like Proverbs says, it's "Out of the abundance of the heart the mouth speaks." That's why people always say what they mean when they don't filter what they say but then turn around and apologize or say they were just kidding.

Whenever there's a heart issue there's a love issue, and whenever there's a love issue there's a people issue.

I believe that's why so many believers, who are just as heartsick as nonbelievers, operate with such a high level of hate, pain, manipulation, and deception. They're just as bound as the nonbeliever because they don't have the capacity to walk in the *freedom* of love. Just as racists are bound, they are bound by hatred. Consequently, the nonbeliever doesn't want anything to do with the God of the believer because the actions of the believer don't demonstrate love; while the believer believes in God, he or she is not walking in the *freedom* of love. An excellent biblical definition of love can be found in I Corinthians 13: 4-8, 13:

4: Love is patient, love is kind. It does not envy, it does not boast, it is not proud.

5: It does not dishonor others, it is not self-seeking, it is not easily angered, it keeps no record of wrongs.

6: Love does not delight in evil but rejoices with the truth.

7: It always protects, always trusts, always hopes, always perseveres.

8: Love never fails. But where there are prophecies, they will cease; where there are tongues, they will be stilled; where there is knowledge, it will pass away.

13. And now these three remain: faith, hope, and love. But the greatest of these is love.

These passages of scripture are a great tool for self-examination and to create awareness so we might walk with greater love in every facet of our lives. Never underestimate the destructive capabilities of a defiled heart. I've come to realize many instances where I demonstrated flawed and inconsistent love. Love is the ultimate characteristic of Jesus, and many of us have not walked in consistent love. Reading the words of Jesus, fasting, and praying will reveal these character flaws every time. We have to become and stay *free* so we can demonstrate love the way Jesus does, *free* from all retaliation.

CHAPTER 3

Break *Free* from Pain

"The high and lofty one who lives in eternity, the Holy One, says this: 'I live in the high and holy place with those whose spirits are contrite and humble. I restore the crushed spirit of the humble and revive the *courage* of those with repentant hearts.'"

~Isaiah 57:15 NLT

Most of us can retell stories about the emotional pain we've experienced. To effectively walk in the vision God has for us, we must be whole and *free* from the pain of our past. So many people suppress their pain and adopt a protective mask instead of completely healing their pain at its core. Indeed, *freedom* from pain would make some lives unrecognizable. Some pain that is deeply rooted will only go away with much prayer and fasting to break the ties of trauma bonding. Other pain may only require minimal therapy.

Masks

I've noticed that many people go through their lives wearing masks. I recognize masks because a person wearing a mask (me) knows a mask when she encounters one. I've always worn masks very well no matter the turmoil, hurt, uncertainty, indecision, or fear I've felt. Wearing a mask is a choice. I justified my decision by thinking it was more important to be a leader and bring God glory no matter how weak or vulnerable I felt. "People have their own problems, so there's no need to share yours; just be a source," is what I often thought to myself. Beyond that, I also thought, "Don't bleed on other people." I believe that's why it felt like a hole in my soul when my two closest friends unexpectedly died within one week of each other in the first week of March 2018. I could be vulnerable with them and vice versa, but who else could I reveal my true self to? Most people see our *strengths* but don't understand we also need a lot of comfort.

God wants us to completely heal from our

past pains so we can become a source of *strength*, strong enough to tell our stories and help others. If we never become *free* from our pain, how can we effectively help others become *free* from theirs? How can we be instruments of change and healing if we are still battling our own past?

On the surface, we can look like a public success but at the same time be a private failure because we refuse to confront and deal with the deeper issues that plague our heart. Don't we understand that if we don't attend to the issues that plague us that our lives are more bound than the people behind prison bars? Imagine that. In other words, we may not be physically restricted but we nonetheless experience a myriad of dysfunctional restrictions in our emotional, mental, and spiritual health. These levels of dysfunctions cause great deterioration of not only the soul but also an individual's moral character, identity, and overall perspective on life.

Heart Issues

Masks are indicative of being bound, and being bound is a by-product of the issues that flow from the heart. These heart issues can impact every area of our lives.

For some people, heart issues manifest in their emotions, mind, desires, hopes, trust, wills, passions, and even their mind-sets. Negative emotions of the heart break up happy homes, breed disloyalty on the job, ruin friendships, harbor grudges, create soul ties, cause rejection of one's self and others, influence us to abandon responsibility, think negatively, operate with poor interpersonal skills, become impatient with and chronically critical of others, and the list goes on for infinity. In Psalms 51:10, David once prayed, "Create in me a clean heart oh Lord and renew a right spirit within me." Proverbs 4:23 NLT says, "Above all else, guard your heart, for everything you do flows from it." KJV says, "Keep thy heart with all diligence; for out of it are the issues of life." NLT says, "Guard your heart above all else, for it determines the course of your life." There are many matters of the heart, but until people examine their own hearts, they'll never truly be *free* in spite of any surface appearance of *freedom* they might enjoy.

Pain should never become the new normal. You have the power to overcome all pain regardless of how severe it is. Marrying pain rather than divorcing it by any means necessary says you value the pain over your health and a better life. Overcoming pain really does start with healthy new ways of healing your heart from the core. For some, this requires very deep spiritual intervention while for others surface therapy delivers just as effectively. We're all genetically and emotionally different when it comes to emotional tolerance. An event might cause one individual to become only mildly depressed while the same event could lead to chronic and severe depression if not suicidal tendencies in someone else. It all boils down to the ability to absorb emotional pain; emotional resilience, tolerance and penetration. For teachable reference, I've nicknamed this emotional absorption capacity (EAC) and will discuss in greater detail in the next couple sections of this chapter.

Spiritual Peace Chain

You have to learn to increase your emotional tolerance just as you have, hopefully, learned to increase your stress tolerance. There are many holistic ways of accomplishing this (such as spending time with God in prayer, meditating on the word of God, fasting, listening to powerful apostolic teachings about God, and worship), but when all those fail, deep, long-term therapy should be considered. Unless you discover the root of the problem and deal with it, you rob yourself of the abundant life God wants you to have. When you uncover revelations about your emotional trauma, you will begin to sever the bond you've built with it. That power to sever the bond can only come from a deeply rooted spiritual place within you.

Turn on your imagination. Visualize your actual heart broken into pieces. In order to hold it together, you must do something different. So, you decide to give your heart a major wrapping. The one-strand cord didn't work because you've tried that for years. Now, you're going to wrap it with a three-strand cord because otherwise it will continue to bleed out and seep through the cord, remaining broken. The three-strand cord you've decided on holds it in place, but the cords have to be all applied at the same time and done consistently to prevent you from returning to that place of emotional trauma. (This application can be found in a real-world example using Lexus' timing belt. They realized the timing chain was sturdier than a timing belt because a belt has to be replaced after so many miles and a chain is stronger and almost unbreakable with its three-strand metal configuration.) You need the same type of fortification in the spiritual. Therapy can provide insight, but it's the spiritual uprooting that goes to the core of your soul to eliminate the residue. This spiritual uprooting is best accomplished through spiritual fasting coupled with intense reading of the Bible and fervent prayer. Think of it as a strategy to hold your heart—the place where your emotions are housed—in place. You need this three-chord fortification and spiritual renewal. Your ability to wrap this "spiritual peace chain" around your heart will allow you to soulfully move forward with your life.

Decreasing Your Emotional Absorption Capacity (EAC)

Once you apply your spiritual peace chain, you'll experience a significant decrease in your emotional absorption capacity for trauma-laced emotions.

You won't find that phrase, "emotional absorption capacity" (EAC), anywhere but here, so don't Google it for clarity. I'll explain it.

I'm sure you've heard expressions like, "let it roll off your back like water on a duck's back" or "what doesn't break you will make you stronger" or "sticks and stones may break my bones but words will never hurt me." These expressions are empowering on the surface but the truth of the matter is that the penetration of some pain is what I call "high absorption." You may feel powerless trying to prevent how deeply emotions hurt, and so you respond in a way that is described this way in the military: "False motivation leads to real motivation." In other words, you expect that if you wear the mask long enough and put on a façade, the pain really does go away. But the truth is that the pain really is buried and it becomes rooted over time. You act it out in many of your behaviors and interactions with others.

Confront Your Pain Head On

That is why you have to deal with your pain by confronting it head on. I heard someone mention how a mass murderer will become frantic if someone runs toward him while he is in the act of shooting, the way cops are trained to do, instead of running away from him. Most people wouldn't do that nor would they have the *courage* to because they're more afraid of getting shot than being *courage*ous enough to charge straight at the shooter and confront him.

You should act the same way when dealing with your emotional pain. It may hurt you but until you confront it, you'll never overcome and conquer it. It will always be negatively impacting your life and binding you to your past with emotional chains causing you to be stuck years into your past. I know many mother-and-daughter relationships that are like this. It's even tried to take root in my own relationship with my mom. There are many types of relationships that are impacted by emotional trauma, and the individuals involved refuse to cope holistically and often turn to alcohol (and become functional alcoholics), drugs, promiscuity, have multiple sex partners, become workaholics, and so many other negative consequences. When people are bound to unhealthy emotions of their past, they consequently bind themselves to even more unhealthy behavioral patterns. Some even have the audacity to highlight these behaviors on social media when, in reality, it's really their way of coping.

How will you become more intentional about healing and decreasing your EAC?

CHAPTER 4

Break *Free* from Unforgiveness

"Then Peter came to him and asked, "Lord, how often should I forgive someone who sins against me? Seven times?" Matthew 18: 21

After leaving the corporate world, I remember realizing that I was still dealing with areas of unforgiveness I wasn't aware of. It wasn't until I stopped, indirectly self-medicating that it was possible for me realize it so I could become whole and live purposefully and spontaneously in his will. This self-medication made me become like Martha. Once I became *free* from "being a Martha" (Martha is a biblical character whose priority was to work hard for Jesus rather than spend quality time with him), building others' ministries, and being a workaholic in the corporate world I became *free* to meditate on the word of God, spend intimate time in noncorporate worship, and discover what was really going on in my heart.

Feelings of not being able to forgive began to bubble up to the surface in my mind and emotions when I learned that my childhood molester was being released from prison. As I dealt with the emotional and perhaps psychological healing of the molestation days before this person was going to be released from prison, it cleared a greater path of communication between God and I. It was then that I opened myself up to receiving God's love at a greater capacity. It was then that I became *free* to really hear God and receive his instruction for the next phase of my life. I had no idea that for many years I had suppressed emotions of anger, rage, and unforgiveness until I heard of this man's impending *freedom*. Up until then I had not thought about the time he had molested me and I had never talked about it.

Sometimes it takes an event to trigger the reality of what we're really feeling.

We often hear about forgiveness, and it's almost a cliché until you discover you're subconsciously holding on to unforgiveness. You discover it is still lurking in your subconscious when something happens to the victimizer and your emotions heighten as the victim. Examples of this would be when your victimizer, who molested you, is released from prison for doing to someone else the very same thing he did to you at the tender age of five, and you decide you want to tell on him now so he's not released and will be brought up on new charges; something bad happens to the ex who hurt you, so you rejoice and become Fox News on social media; the boss who always hindered your progress gets hurt on the job and can't come to work for a while, and you throw a mini corporate party.

The saying, "Hurt people hurt people," is actually true, so you have to discover a way to forgive the person who hurt you and move past the hurt. You should pray for the person who hurt you while asking God to help you to become *free* from the trauma bonding and painful emotions you've been carrying. A significant amount of emotional trauma bonding occurs when there is rejection; adult or childhood wounds from verbal, physical, or sexual abuse; infidelity instead of loyalty; and abandonment. Honestly, you will never get all the apologies you deserve from people, so you might need to become the bigger person and apologize just for peace's sake regardless of your being right or wrong. Choosing the relationship over the principle of the matter is a conscious decision. Be grateful our Heavenly Father didn't choose the principle of the matter when it came to us and how we once hurt and rejected him.

The side effects of your state of not forgiving don't really manifest until you're around someone who reminds you of the offender.

The pain is still there because, in your mind, the offense is still there, and you haven't forgiven the offender.

Sometimes, the offender will never ask for your forgiveness, and you will just have to make up your mind that you will no longer be bound by unforgiveness. Challenge yourself to really forgive by using Christ like love.

Forgiveness is not letting the person who hurt you off the hook. Quite frankly, they're most likely already *free* and going on with their own life, if not deceased and gone on to glory. In fact, your oppressor might not even remember the incident so burned into your soul! You owe it to yourself to be *free* from those negative emotions so you, too, can move on with your life. The pain you experienced was a part of your growing process and testing for the impact you can have at the next level of your existence so you could help others become *free* so they live their best lives in the present moment.

You are not what you've been through; you're who you pull other victims through.

Another major door of unforgiveness is opened through rejection. What helps me forgive those who have rejected me is when I think of how much rejection my Abba Father, Jesus, experienced. Sometimes, I embrace rejection as a means of getting to know God in the fellowship of his suffering as the Bible mentions. Rejection is also a very common form of pain you could be experiencing in a current relationship.

Rejection negatively affects your joy and self-confidence, but it should never penetrate your emotions to the point you reject yourself, experiencing low self-esteem.

Free yourself from this emotional turmoil by filling your mind with positive affirmation, spending more time with nontoxic people who celebrate and not just tolerate you. Meet new people through new networking groups, holiday drop-ins, and positive social media clubs. Understand you're uniquely amazing and so is your tribe of genuine relators. See yourself in powerful new and healthy relationships that empower you to become your best self as a result of breaking *free* from the unforgiveness and rejection. These relationships allow you to receive regular withdrawals of support for at least as much as the positive deposits you put into them.

You also expand your mental capacity and allow yourself to meditate on the positive so you become more productive. Multiple studies show happier people are much more productive. You will no longer be self-destructive or self-sabotaging, with negative thought chatters and private pity parties.

There are two scriptures that have really kept me *free* from unforgiveness. In Psalms 51:10, when David says, "Create in me a clean heart O God and renew the right spirit in me," and when Jesus declared as he hung on the cross, "Lord, forgive them for they know not what they do." These scriptures keep me humble and in a greater state of forgiveness in my love walk.

CHAPTER 5

Break Free from the "In-a-Me"

"Stop pointing fingers at the enemy and accept full responsibility for your self-sabotaging ways, your in-a-me." Shateka Husser

Many Christians blame circumstances and situations on the enemy, alluding to satanic or spiritual warfare as the cause for their failures, disappointments, or setbacks. There are many cases of this ignorance. We must be sensitive to embracing the harsh reality of our own sabotage, careful not to allow it to go on for extended periods of time.

When we blame everything on the enemy when the fault is really the "in-a-me" (ourselves) we never own the resulting failures or disappointments.

Using the enemy as a scapegoat keeps us stagnant, never reaching our full potential. Instead we should seek greater solutions and ways to execute more effectively.

We also fail because God strategically allows things to happen because he chastens those he loves. People give the enemy too much credit. We have to stop looking to the external and look to the internal. It's not about what someone did to you or the lemons life deals you, it's about looking deeper within and really evaluating how you could have showed up, executed, negotiated, moved, or responded differently to get a more desirable result. Ownership is everything so take full responsibility.

This becomes extremely important when we start discussing stewardship over the assignment and purpose God has planned for us to execute. In the army, they always said, "excuses are tools of incompetence, and those who specialize in them specialize in nothing else." So, we were never allowed an excuse of any magnitude. Even if there was a reason, it was never justifiable. You figured it out, and you made it happen by any means necessary. When we begin to take that approach and accept full responsibility for every relationship, career, education, business, ministry, or organization we influence, partner with, or lead, we will experience a recognizably different and better result.

Identity Crisis

For many years, I was in crisis mode with many others. I knew what I was born into and who I wanted to become. I felt I did pretty well in the great roles and opportunities I was afforded in both personal and professional aspects of my life but I didn't always do as well when it came to certain assignments God presented. I didn't always prioritize those divine assignments like I should have. I remember taking over the largest store, in terms of square footage, of this particular supercenter chain in South Carolina, and a prophet telling me, "not only will your leadership transform this place in the physical realm, it will also transform it in the spiritual." Although my team and I made substantial improvements in every aspect of the store's operation, culture, and appearance, things would have been that much greater had I been walking in my kingdom identity (representing as God's ambassador). I didn't understand how much more growing I needed to do to effectively fight through all the spiritual warfare I was experiencing because I was lacking in Biblical knowledge and consequently spiritual power.

I was created to lead although I never had a desire to. From being the oldest of three children to leading America's sons and daughters as an army officer to leading hundreds in corporate environments, and yes, even leading in churches. I've done it all well, but all these leadership roles weren't my God-given purpose. They were all roles of preparation for whom God was cultivating me to be. He was always the potter and I was just the clay he was shaping and molding, according to Isaiah 64:8. Now, I understand the many transitions I had to make. Now, I understand the many character tests I had to pass. Now, I understand why he had to move me for my continued growth and before my soul became contaminated in certain shifting environments. Now, I understand the fervency he had for my quicker than anticipated transitions because as soon as I felt close to mastering a situation, he sent me signs to shift. He was always keeping me humble when he made me start over and build from scratch once again, confident only in him. It was all because he was building me to become.... The ideal role is the one that he has shown me while thirsting for more of him. I finally found my identity when I fasted and prayed and just waited. Some people, I assume, were on a quicker path to discovering their identity, but I had to labor many years to understand mine. We all have different paths, and we all have our own unique identities and growth patterns. Now, I understand why I went through the hell I endured from toddler until adulthood.

I didn't just go through it; I had to grow through it to be prepared.

Some identities, especially those that are divine, require tremendous growth, integrity, wisdom, and stamina to attain. My destiny, my identity, and my impact were always what the enemy sought to destroy along with those of many of my spiritual brothers and sisters. I'm just super grateful that, in my wilderness, in my lost moments, God did not allow me to be consumed by evil. I truly understand what Romans 8:28 means when it says, "All things work together for the good," but I like the NLT version better: "And we know that God causes everything to work together for the good of those who love God and are called according to His purpose for them."

"If God be for you, who can be against you," became my motto during those extreme times when people were trying to assassinate my reputation. When you don't know who you, you indulge in behaviors that are far beneath you and below the royal inheritance God has in store for you. Even if it were done with good intentions, if done unwisely, your actions could be detrimental to your reputation. Then there were those times when you really were carnal for a moment. For example, you might have retaliated instead of fighting through prayer and worship. Additionally, not only do you sabotage your kingdom identity but you also lose spiritual authority and *strength* when you react in these carnal ways. Reacting causes you to leak spiritual power just like a car battery loses power when the headlights are left on.

It's important to know who you are so you don't allow fear to drive your response; instead, you allow faith to drive you. You see, we are a generation that is called to be in covenant with God and that requires holy living. 1 Peter 2:9, KJV says,

"But ye are a chosen generation, a royal priesthood, a holy nation, a peculiar people; that ye should shew forth the praises of him who hath called you out of darkness into his marvelous light."

Perfection may seem far out of reach, but excellence is achieved when we are passionate about our identity. It's not until then that real vision is birthed and creativity is produced.

When you lack an identity, you will always lack a dream. Now, I understand why I never really had a real dream. I didn't have a vision. I remember thinking while still working in the corporate world, "I've traveled to fifteen countries; I've served my country, reached a level of corporate success; now all I can think to dream of is becoming a helpmate for my husband."

Boy, was I wrong. God had a different, major plan for me. He invested too much into me for me to think so little of whom I was. I'm not downplaying the wife role, but God had a different plan for my dream that I didn't have. His dream for me became mine. Sometimes, after reaching a level of success, you plateau when you don't have identity and vision. It's the difference between a thought and reality. The Bible says people perish because they lack vision. They become unfruitful and unable to be used by God as a result. My prayer is that if you don't already have a vision, you begin to understand who you are. When you lack vision, you are so busy serving others you have no clue who you were really created to be.

For many years and through many transitions, I've served in every capacity you can think of in a church. I was working for the Lord but around some of the most hateful, unloving people I could have ever been around. I did it anyway because I loved God and out of worship to him, I continued to work alongside these people. They obviously didn't know who they were, either. In some cases, they were more hateful than the people in my professional workplace. I've experienced church leaders talking about church members and other leaders so I was clear what my role was in these organizations, intercession. Behind the scenes, I found myself running interference between the congregants and the leaders of the congregation coupled with prayer. So, I had a level of knowledge when it came to my kingdom identity, but I didn't understand the totality of whom I was.

Spending time with God will reveal all things. When you understand your true identity, you understand why certain scenarios had to play out the way they did in your life. You understand why it was so extremely hard to become *free* from bondage. You understand why your relationships patterned themselves the way they did, and you understand so much more. You understand why and how you've sabotaged yourself in certain situations. Most important, you understand how important it was for things to occur so you could be better equipped for your greater purpose.

Focus

Broken fellowship with God will always create a misalignment of focus because your mind is constantly cluttered with competing nonpriorities.

Your focus has to be saturated with purposefully positive initiatives. You usually find those initiatives when you've determined who you are.

Your "who" is way more important than your "why." If you don't know who you are, your why is wrong, anyway.

A great way to bring your mind back into alignment is by remaining prayerful and even fasting when necessary. Constant dialogue with the Father will help your focus when you make room and time to hear his gentle voice. The more time you spend with him, the better you will become at recognizing his voice. He said, "My sheep know my voice and another they will not follow." In other words, my followers won't allow demonic activity to distract them from focusing on what I intend them to do, the purpose I have for them.

Once you figure out your identity and determine your God-given purpose, your actions toward its fulfillment, on a scale of 1 to 10, will become a 20. You see how that works: Your purpose is the assignment revealed to you once you become clear on your identity.

"Stinking Thinking"—Overcoming Fear

One thing is for sure: Once you become clear on your assignment, you have to constantly feed your faith because all types of warfare are released against your mind.

By the term warfare, I'm referring to the innumerable doubts and fears caused by your inner critic and negative thought chatters. One of the greatest books I've ever read on the subject was written by Joyce Meyer, Battlefield of the Mind. I remember that being my gift to about a dozen people while stationed in Germany. If you're like me, you can en*courage* everyone else, but you struggle to en*courage* yourself. You sit there and allow the darts to be fired at you internally. You have to fight back with the word of God. You have to speak the word of God for every dart thrown at you by your demons. Your faith has to be stronger than your fears.

Your faith should be connected to your heart, which is connected to your mouth. In other words, you should always be speaking truth and decreeing a different result. Proverb 23:7

says, "As a man thinketh in his heart so is he (or she)." Saying words of affirmation, writing down your vision, and taking intentional actions will yield a different manifestation. "Give your faith an assignment" is something I've heard Apostle John Eckhardt say. We should be dispatching our angels on a continual basis. I just believe your angels are greater than your demons. Just like I believe our God, in his omnipotence, is more powerful and greater than any problem we focus our faith and attention on.

Whether it's fear of the unknown, fear of failure, or fear of negative consequences, you can never move forward when you are afraid. Show me a person who procrastinates or hesitates and I could most likely show you fear. Jonah was afraid. I'm sure Joseph was very afraid when he was thrown into the pit. The three Hebrew boys, Shadrach, Meshach, and Abednego had a level of fear when they went into the fiery furnace. There are countless biblical stories where *courage* had to overcome fear.

You often hear stories of people who are afraid of doing something being told to do it anyway. I jumped five times out of a perfectly good airplane; it was my first five times ever even flying in a plane. I was much younger, but I knew the Holy Spirit was with me, and I had more faith in him than my parachute. No matter where we go in life or what we have to go through, there's always a level of fear. I'll be honest; up until this year, I used to be afraid of getting married. Besides seeing the alarming rates of divorce in and out of the church, I experienced married men making passes at me so I subconsciously developed a disrespect for me. Additionally, I did not have a father figure and many of the men I encountered, including some in my family, were cheaters. I felt infidelity was inevitable since Holy Spirit couldn't even tame the men in the church, and I never wanted to sign up for a broken heart.

We all have fears, but when we begin to trust in our God who's most powerful, we slam the door on fear. Fear is torment. It's the devil. It's not at all a healthy emotion, and we have to deal with it in order to live a life of *freedom*. No matter what, we should have an undeniable hope in Jesus instead of expecting the negative. Fear keeps you in a cave, never lets you out around people. Fear keeps you muzzled without allowing the world to hear your voice. It hinders you for no good reason. Fumigate this "stinking thinking"!

Stress and Depression

The vicious cycle of choosing worry over faith is commonly known as stress. It is not a good look or feel. The anxiety that manifests from experiencing so much **stress** can cause poor communication, self-sabotaging behaviors, memory loss, poor concentration, and the list goes on and on. Most important, it can cause health issues.

Simply put, depression is concentrating on what we don't have rather than being grateful for what we do have.

Although I did not allow it to manifest, I found myself about to become depressed on many occasions this past year as a result of not having my two closest friends around. They unexpectedly died within one week of each other. They lived in Georgia and South Carolina and did not know each other except for one brief meeting at my birthday party almost four years ago.

What helps alleviate depression is to have the power to shift your focus. From a spiritual standpoint, the Holy Spirit can help in this area when you spend more time with God. I've found worship to be the one activity that brings me to a more centered, calm, and serene environment.

Worship for me is what yoga and meditation are to the secular world. It allows me to release stress because in His presence is fullness of joy. These atmospheres are saturated with comfort and peace.

Depression has some neurological impact as well, and I've found that St. John's Wort helps with chemical imbalances and mood. I used to jokingly prescribe it to my direct reports when I was a leader in the corporate world, and some even went as far to take me up on it and found it worked, but I always warned them that I wasn't a mental health professional although I've studied a great about it. Exercising, eating the right foods (consuming less sugar), and getting sufficient amounts of vitamin D from sunlight are some of the natural ways of fighting depression. It's important to know how to combat depression because it slows down your productivity and effectiveness when it comes to your purpose. We have too much to do to allow this hindrance in our lives.

Focusing more on others than on yourself is probably one of the most effective ways to combat depression.

The one thing that keeps me out of the depression zone is to not allow it to get a foothold in my spirit. If you let the devil ride, he will always take over and drive. Depression is arguably not all spiritual, but it does affect your soul, and I've found my spiritual *strength* to have a direct impact on and manifest in my emotional and mental well-being.

To further testify, after leaving Iraq and experiencing the nightmares, the fears of riding under overpasses, I was diagnosed with PTSD. That's short for post-traumatic stress disorder. You can get it so many ways that people don't discuss, from being molested, verbal or physical abuse, the death of loved ones, and many other traumatic events. I personally believe it also manifested as a greater level of cluster phobias because, for example, I never used to have an issue with elevators.

However, I didn't want to accept this diagnosis until it became evident during certain stressful situations. I continued to work and handle my business as if I did not have it. That's when I discovered St. John's Wort to be of benefit. I took it periodically after I abruptly stopped taking prescribed medication after six months of use. My stomach couldn't take it anymore and after experiencing the vomiting, I stopped taking it cold turkey. Again, everyone's body is different, and people should follow their doctors' orders, but I believe God miraculously took me off those meds healing me from the PTSD. I do have moments ever so often, but that's when my spiritual status is imbalanced.

I honestly believe there are a tremendous number of people who have moments of mental challenges, just as any other medical sickness, but have never been properly diagnosed. I can't prove it, but my keen discernment has led me to believe that. I've experienced and seen a lot of the signs of mental instability in people I've been in relationships with in the workplace and church and even noticed these signs from a distance in one of our major national leaders whose name goes without saying.

When I feel mental illness trying to attack, at the onset, I steal away and get into his presence because in his presence there is fullness of joy and divine healing. He is Jehovah Rapha, the Lord of healing, and I'm convinced that if he did it before he can do it again. He's the same God!

I believe that not only depression, but all types of health issues are demonic tactics or ways to keep the believer immobilized from working in his or her kingdom-driven purpose, to frustrate and abort the will of God. I decree and declare that every spirit of infirmity has to go, and then we will be victorious to live out our God-given dreams. We will not die but live and declare the work of the Lord (Psalm 118:7). We will not take our dream to the grave, but we will release it on earth for generations to come. We will do greater works beyond these slight afflictions. Many are the afflictions of the righteous, but our Savior delivers us from them all (Psalms 34:19). When the enemy comes in like a flood, Jesus always comes and lifts a standard in us (Isaiah 59:19). He causes us to triumph because in him, we are more than conquerors.

I've heard a few testimonies about people in comas who came out of them because healing scriptures were read to them. I know we did the same for a cousin of mine who was in an almost two-month coma after suffering severe head trauma from a deadly motorbike accident. He's perfectly fine today. There are hundreds more stories like this one, and here are a few healing scriptures to read:

Exodus 15:26: "If you diligently heed the voice of the LORD your God and do what is right in His sight, give ear to His commandments and keep all His statutes, I will put none of the diseases on you which I have brought on the Egyptians. For I am the LORD who heals you."

Exodus 23:25: "So you shall serve the LORD your God, and He will bless your bread and your water. And I will take sickness away from the midst of you."

2 Kings 20:5: "Return and tell Hezekiah the leader of My people, 'Thus says the LORD, the God of David your father: I have heard your prayer, I have seen your tears; surely I will heal you. On the third day you shall go up to the house of the LORD.'"

2 Chronicles 7:14: "If My people who are called by My name will humble themselves and pray and seek My face, and turn from their wicked ways, then I will hear from heaven, and will forgive their sin and heal their land."

Psalm 6:2: "Have mercy on me, O LORD, for I am weak; O LORD, heal me, for my bones are troubled."

Psalm 30:2: "O LORD my God, I cried out to You, and you healed me.

Psalm 41:1-3: "Blessed is he who considers the poor; the LORD will deliver him in time of trouble. The Lord will preserve him and keep him alive, and he will be blessed on the earth; You will not deliver him to the will of his enemies. The LORD will *strength*en him on his bed of illness; You will sustain him on his sickbed."

Psalm 103:2-3: "Bless the LORD, O my soul, and forget not all His benefits; Who forgives all your iniquities; who heals all your diseases."

Psalm 107:20: "He sent His word and healed them..."

Proverbs 3:7-8: "Do not be wise in your own eyes; fear the LORD and depart from evil. It will be health to your flesh, and *strength* to your bones."

Proverbs 4:20-22: "My son, give attention to my words; incline your ear to my sayings. Do not let them depart from your eyes; keep them in the midst of your heart; for they are life to those who find them, and health to all their flesh."

Prophecy to Yourself

This section is about mind-set and believing in yourself. I believe in looking in the mirror and prophesying to myself. I will not wait on a prophet. I will read the word and declare God's word over my life, and you should do the same. It's not enough to just speak it consistently, though. You have to believe. Sometimes God will still move in spite of your unbelief. He's done it for me in a big way, so I would do you a disservice to say God will not move in a nonbeliever. However, he does move quicker when you believe. It's impossible to please him without believing in him, but because of his favor and according to His will, He'll move things in your favor. He loves to manifest the seemingly impossible because He loves to be glorified. He's not like man. We do ourselves a disservice when we expect little. When I understood this, I literally nicknamed myself Confidently Favored on Facebook because when I wasn't worthy, He did it anyway. When I didn't believe, He did it anyway. He moves when he wants to, how he wants to, for whom he chooses and doesn't need permission from anyone.

So I say, prophecy over yourself. David was one who had to en*courage* himself in the Lord. He was a king who received tremendous favor from God in spite of his sins and hang-ups. God doesn't have favorites. The same way he showed up for David, he has showed up for us, humanity, when we didn't deserve it. The thing we must understand about prophecy is we must have spiritual authority. Spiritual authority comes with living in close relationship with God, living a sin-*free* life; we become like Moses, a friend of God. It's that same level of relationship that allows us to intercede in prayer on someone's behalf and have our prayers answered because of our favor with God. Sometimes, sinners know more about our favor than we do. They'll ask for our prayers as if we were a priest or something because they're clear they don't have a relationship or aren't in a relationship with God like they know they should be, so instead of simply repenting, they would rather use a seemingly righteous believer to pray on their behalf.

Make your decree and speak it consistently regardless of how big or small. There was a time I could not see my own beauty because one of my relatives said I was ugly and I believed her. Then I would always say to her how beautiful I was without waiting for her validation, even when I didn't see it. I kept doing this until it actually manifested and I saw my own beauty. As I said before, false motivation will turn into real motivation.

The two most profound ways you can minister to yourself and build yourself up instead of allowing the "in-a-me" to prevail is to prophesy (Romans 4:17) to yourself and pray in the Holy Spirit according to Jude 1:20 and Romans 8:26..

CHAPTER 6

Break *Free* from Addictions

"And lead us not into temptation, but deliver us from the evil one." Matthew 6:13

Many people have addictions and they manifest in various forms. The problem with addictions is that they become priorities and distract or derail people from purposeful living. These are manifestations of not having enough discipline to stop or significantly decrease an activity because of sensational, uncontrollable desires. Many of these desires become destructive because they're modern forms of idolatry and

God hates idolatry. He is a jealous God as stated numerous times throughout the old scriptures, and his character has not changed. He will let no addiction or idolatry come before him.

To break free from addictions, we need to declare and experience a heart change.

"Thy word have I hid in my heart that I may not sin against thee," Psalms 119:11.

The most common addictions today are our use of social media, lying, sex, porn, drinking, drugs, stealing, gossiping, fighting, gambling, shopping, and even traveling. Again, these serve as barriers to purposeful living when indulged in excessively or immorally. They significantly derail you from achieving the vision God has for your life. When the word of God is digested on a regular basis, coupled with prayer and fasting, any addiction can be broken. You may have to read scripture until you feel him. You may have to read scripture until you understand it, like anything else you study. You may have to pray until you feel his presence. You may have to worship and wait in his presence until you feel glory. The one thing you need to help you overcome any addiction is his Holy Spirit because where the Holy Spirit is, there is conviction to such immorality or time wasters.

A person without conviction is a dangerous person to be around.

Their unfruitful demons will leach onto you and before you know it, if you're not the stronger one, you too will be engaging in the same activities. It's wise to simply stay away from demons you're not strong enough to fight. Ephesians 4:27 says "Neither give place to the devil." James 4:7 says "Submit yourselves therefore to God. Resist the devil, and he will flee from you."

Carefully Guard Your Spirit

Some of these addictions may not affect you, but if you struggle with the same addictions as the other person or you're not strong enough to be around their demons, and especially if there's immoral sexual chemistry, then be wise and refer the individual to one of your respected spiritual leaders. Don't take on more than you can bear or it will lead to your own demise. So sometimes, you might have to sever ties from a person, not to offend or make the person feel bad, but to maintain your *sanctification* and relationship with Christ. It's imperative not to jeopardize our spiritual *strength* because of the unyielding, charismatic, demonic activity of others.

People should spiritually inspire you, not expire you.

You may have to fast, on their behalf, until they shift their behavior, but don't jeopardize your walk with God and purpose for their company. Such reprobate spirits are contagious and detrimental to walking out the purpose of God. Anyone who is lukewarm and without passion toward God's purpose for his or her life by choice or ignorance is a person who needs to receive the fullness of Holy Spirit, experience new revelation, and discipled for greater understanding.

God will always send the right company to walk beside you on your purpose journey but many times He allows a season of isolation or separation until you are clear about your season, identity or purpose. This is super important because when the fiery darts come your way—notice, I didn't say if, but when—you'll have a firm enough foundation to be steadfast in purpose according to I Corinthians 15:58: "Therefore, my dear brothers and sisters, stand firm. Let nothing move you. Always give yourselves fully to the work of the Lord, because you know that your labor in the Lord is not in vain."

You won't waver as a result of being unsure, but you will accomplish what he sends you to do according to Romans 8:28: "And we know that in all things God works for the good of those who love him, who have been called according to his purpose."

The Relationship between Evangelism and Addiction

There was a time in my younger walk with Christ when I would attempt to evangelize the opposite sex because I was passionate about saving souls. But I didn't understand that their demons were stronger than my spirit because I lacked power as a result of not having enough depth in the word nor had my full armor on as discussed in Ephesians 6:13-17: Wherefore take unto you the whole armor of God, that ye may be able to withstand in the evil day, and having done all, to stand. "Stand therefore, having your loins girt about with truth, and having on the breastplate of righteousness: And your feet shod with the preparation of the gospel of peace; and above all, taking the shield of faith, wherewith ye shall be able to quench all the fiery darts of the devil. And take the helmet of *salvation*, and the sword of the Spirit, which is the word of God." This lack prevented me from using the sword of the Holy Spirit, which is having the word on the inside. This malfunction of my sword prevented me from fighting the temptations of others as well as my own. My helmet of *salvation*, which gives our minds the discernment, wisdom, and insight to understand the tactics and deception of the enemy, wasn't on properly. I didn't put on the breastplate of righteousness as a result of not setting boundaries. I didn't tap into the word of God on the inside to keep me strong enough to fight the temptations encountered from his devil. I didn't know how expensive this encounter would be, contaminating my mind, will, and emotions. So, I was essentially opening a door to the enemy. We all know, according to Luke 11:26, "He brings seven more demons with him." These are sexually transmitted demons that create soul ties as a result of the intercourse. That's an entire lesson for another book but research incubus and succubus demons on YouTube or Google. The scriptures tell us they come back with even more evil spirits, or demons, than before. Luke 11:24, 26, says,

"When an evil spirit leaves a person, it goes into the desert, searching for rest. But when it finds none, it says, 'I will return to the person I came from. Then the spirit finds seven other spirits more evil than itself, and they all enter the person and live there. And so that person is worse off than before.'"

The breastplate of righteousness has to be so solid that temptation can't pierce, penetrate, or overtake us, especially when I Corinthians 10:13 says, "He will make a way of escape." I was overtaken in my vulnerability and fell into what many have called "missionary dating." It was a tactic of the enemy to keep me bound even though I had good intentions.

There are seasons when your freedom looks like deliverance but that's only because you weren't presented with strategic temptations.

Don't be fooled and bamboozled. Stay guarded.

It is often said it takes twenty-one days to break a habit. This is essentially saying it takes twenty-one days to break an addiction-saturated activity. I suggest going even further and saying that it takes up to ninety days to break a habit or an addiction. From my personal experience, twenty-one days has never been enough time to make a change in any area I desired to change. Of course, the period of abstinence is different for everyone. Not indulging in the activity that we want to change allows us to significantly decrease if not completely eliminate the behavior.

Accountability Partner

Addictions aren't always a negative if you have the ability to overcompensate in other areas. For example, if you make a significant amount of money, indulging in more than usual shopping is not an issue during that time. However, most addictions are destructive and require change in order for a person to be set *free* from a negative cycle. Addictions are weakened when you don't engage in them, but it's wise to be aggressive in your intentionality. It's not enough for you to be intentional and alone in the journey to *freedom* from addictions. This requires having an active, not passive, accountability partner. An accountability partner is someone who keeps you from breaking commitment or covenant. Some spouses even have accountability partners to ensure they stay out of infidelity. It's one thing to hold yourself accountable but having that extra check and balance in place demonstrates another level of intentionality. I believe the enemy causes division among believers so they're prevented from being accountable to one another as commanded in James 5: 6 NLT: "Confess your sins to each other and pray for each other so that you may be healed. The earnest prayer of a righteous person has great power and produces wonderful results."

The Power of the Mind

So how can you overcome any addiction since addictions have the ability to ruin lives, placing people in bondage instead of *freedom*? Every addiction can be ended when a person's mind becomes stronger than the desire. The mind is more powerful than most people give it credit. The mind will play out the disadvantages and negative consequences of the addiction. The mind will give a person a way of escaping from the urge with creative new replacement activities or substitutes. The mind will show a person the destructive consequences before the person resumes indulging in the activity. The mind will not allow the person to even start the addiction. Every act of addiction is always played out first in the imagination before the act is committed even when it's impulsively motivated. In this way, the power of the mind can help people break *free* of their addictions.

CHAPTER 7

Break *Free* from "Soul Ties"

"Beloved, I wish above all things that thou mayest prosper and be in health, *even as thy soul prospereth.*" 3 John 1:2

The *soul* is our *tangible* interaction with the world via our mind, will, and emotion. The spirit is our intangible interaction with God. *Soul* ties are firm grips of stagnation and impairment negatively affecting our mind, will (purpose), and emotions. They're formed from our past, significant involvement with a person (usually through sex) or an organization. It forms when we have sex because of the immediate emotional impact of taking on that person's personality traits as the two of you become one through intercourse. However, soul ties can be formed without sex with anything or anyone you've allowed to take root in your heart and mind.

You can have soul ties to leaders you've worked with in business or those you've served with in nonprofit organizations such as a church. You take on the spirit of your leaders, and many times their struggles become your struggles. For example, as a young army officer and then corporate leader, I took on the spirit of being very unsympathetic because all my leaders were like that. I formed my leadership style by imitating theirs because after experiencing a very dysfunctional childhood, they were my role models. They were effective and successful, and it just seemed the "right" way to be. It wasn't until I had a very empathetic leader that I realized my style was so wrong and really a result of poor people skills as well as setting a negative Christian example. In other instances, when I served under spiritual leaders who've significantly struggled with pride, then I, too began to experience greater degrees of it in my own life.

Soul ties will usually impact your soul by restricting your will, mind, and emotions after you adopt the character traits of those you've spent some level of intimacy, not limited to sex.

The term "tie" suggests you are being restricted and in bondage to the same struggles others have. These ties can subconsciously and deeply transform you.

That's why it's so important that you understand the spirit of a person and uproot any ties that might be forming when you've determined that these ties have strongholds or sins that will make you compromise your values and your purpose.

These ties distract you from your walk with Christ and from hearing his next divine direction for you. You must understand and determine what behaviors are nonnegotiable and unacceptable in the spirit of the people you spend time with and have some level of intimacy with. This is why it is so difficult to sever ties with many friendships. You still love the people you've been in a level of covenant with, especially those friendships of many years, but you no longer desire to compromise your growth for company. Your spiritual maturity outgrew the relationship and consequently you grew apart.

It hurts, but it's a necessary evil for properly accelerating your transformation.

My greatest and most effective way of severing unhealthy ties is not an example I can recommend. With one of my spiritual gifts being mercy, I could almost never muster up the willpower to just sever ties. So, since I couldn't do it in my own *strength*, God would always help me out, but abruptly. This would leave me broken with great pain.

Unfortunately, I'm guilty of returning to toxic relationships out of love, exercising my gift of mercy, and sheer desire for company during times of *sanctification* when I should have remained focused.

I used to compromise to have companionship out of dread or fear of being alone.

I've had to go beyond my soul and tap into my spirit. I understand what Paul was saying when he talked about struggling to do the will of the Father in Romans 7:15-20: "I know that nothing good lives in me, that is, in my flesh; for I have the desire to do what is good, but I cannot carry it out. For I do not do the good I want to do. Instead, I keep on doing the evil I do not want to do. And if I do what I do not want, it is no longer I who do it, but it is sin living in me that does it...." Until I consecrated in prayer and fasting, I was not victorious in the area of soul ties. I had to abandon those ties to live and experience new joys.

Ties cannot be severed by distance or time. Ties can only be severed in spiritual warfare. It's like a fight with the enemy that you are not strong enough to fight in your flesh as stated in II Corinthians 10:4 KJV: "For the weapons of our warfare are not carnal, but mighty through God for the destruction of strongholds." Soul ties are just that, strongholds bonding you to undesired emotions because they plague your mind. Until you can meditate on the word of God concerning the truth as it relates to your struggle, you will never be able to loosen the grip of this demonic force that comes to strip you of your forward momentum and divine destiny. Meditating on the word instead of the soul tie isn't natural or human, it's spiritual, and it might require much fasting.

Break Free from Sexual Sins by any Means Necessary

"God's will is for you to be holy, so stay away from all sexual sin. Then each of you will control his own body and live in holiness and honor— not in lustful passion like the pagans who do not know God and his ways. Therefore, anyone who refuses to live by these rules is not disobeying human teaching but is rejecting God, who gives his Holy Spirit to you."

~1 Thessalonians 4:3-5, 8 NLT

CHAPTER 8

Break Free from Employment Bondage

"And Moses and Aaron came in unto Pharaoh, and said unto him, Thus saith the LORD God of the Hebrews, How long wilt thou refuse to humble thyself before me? let my people go, that they may serve me." Exodus 10:3

Bondage comes in many forms, and one of the primary forms I've seen and experienced is the bondage of employment. It's no secret that, like many people, each of my life's major transitions was in pursuit of more time *freedom*. I left the military then the corporate world searching for more *freedom*, but always for *freedom* to do God's will with less restrictions. It was absolutely my decision to leave the military, but it was absolutely God's collaboration with my carnal bosses to make my work environment so uncomfortable that I wanted to leave the corporate world. While I felt a tug in my spirit to leave, Leviathan's control caused me to be more in control of my *freedom* rather than surrender to God's will and the unknown. In other words, I never had enough faith to abruptly leave when it came to my corporate employment. However, every time—and I can think of three occasions that immediately come to mind—when I prayed and asked God to show me a way out, he did. In fact, he moved rather swiftly in each scenario. I never wanted to leave on my own accord—for example, in switching churches—and I always requested his divine intervention before making moves.

I'll briefly discuss one of my transitions from my last corporate role, which is where I experienced the greatest level of bondage. The bondage was both physical and spiritual; many even nicknamed the facility, "the plantation," as I later learned.

I moved from Charleston, South Carolina, where I'm from to join a corporate leadership team in Baltimore, Maryland. I was super excited to move to the Northeast for the first time to the centrally located Baltimore community that was less than two hours from New Jersey, Philadelphia, and Washington, DC, and only three hours from New York City. Totally unexpected and almost immediately, things began to go wrong in ways that I would never have imagined. I want you to know up front that I now know there was a purpose and plan in all of this, but as I was going through it, it didn't feel that way. I ended up working nights, and I was working so much that I couldn't go to church because I was at work even on Sundays.

My job consumed my life, and I didn't feel joy and fulfillment. In fact, I didn't feel like I was making any impact at all. I remember thinking, "The money is great, but I'm literally working like a slave, and these employees look like they're on a plantation." The way the fulfillment center was set up, I knew it was modern-day slavery. First of all, I was working fourteen hours a day, walking sometimes as much as ten miles per shift because it was a million-square-foot facility, and I was in charge of the entire inbound operation. I felt like I was on a spinning hamster wheel. I was moving and moving and moving but going nowhere.

I became frustrated with the way my life was going. I found myself thinking to God, "I know you have a greater plan than this!" I was living in a wilderness I didn't think I signed up for. I was in a place where I knew no one and where I had no opportunity to really meet anyone because of how much I was working; I was even working for the first time in my life overnight. I began feeling alone and confused about my future. I also remember saying to some of my previous spiritual leaders and thinking to myself, "I have no clue what I'm doing here but I trust God." I also remember thinking, according to Mark 8:36, "What profits a man to gain the whole world and lose their soul," and I knew I hadn't signed up to sell my soul to the devil. But that's how I was feeling, without any trace of purpose.

In my previous role as supercenter store manager with a big box retailer, Walmart, I was given a great level of autonomy to delegate to achieve success, and I did just that. I had delegated my way out of having to work weekends and shifts longer than eight hours. I led an incredible team and was extremely blessed. The grass is not always greener on the other side. Walmart ensured that every individual was treated with a great level of respect and rewarded for his or her achievements. Leaders were empowered to make decisions within their facility to such an extent that we were like mini entrepreneurs running our own supercenters. The work culture allowed me greater *freedom* to serve in purpose.

Getting back to this corporate role, the first

boss I worked with was super difficult and my struggle was real. For the first time, I felt the same way many of my previous direct reports probably felt about me. To be completely honest and transparent, I felt like I was getting a dose of my own medicine that I dished out in moments of stress and frustration when communicating with my previous team. However, I felt relieved and favored when God moved this boss out even though the next boss was no better. In fact, I had to train him. He was from India and had been raised in a culture where women weren't really allowed to speak and have opinions. I didn't feel like I could get my points across, and our interactions created a hostile work environment. Everything he did felt like it was done purposely to degrade me. I didn't want to live my life oppressed; that is never what I would sign up to do. I was created for so much more.

Now I can see that God allowed him to frustrate me to action.

It was not his demons but rather God allowing him to make it so uncomfortable that it would drive me back to the vision board of my life. I began to try and make sense of why I had really been transitioned to Baltimore.

It wasn't much later when I was traveling on a Chicago train I heard a voice say clearly to me, "I brought you to Baltimore to be more." I didn't fully understand that because I didn't have enough vision (of my future) to understand it. God has a way of dripping small bite-sized communications called "a word of knowledge." They require you to seek him out more to gain a fuller understanding. That's exactly what I have done for the majority of this past year, 2018. (I finally feel like I have greater vision after implementing my 8W Clarity Method. I will release those details in another book.)

I would never have sought him without that season of being uncomfortable. It required me to become uncomfortable enough to want change and to do whatever it took to get back to a state of peace. This corporate role was the vehicle God chose to move me to a season of *sanctification* where I would become more like the biblical character Mary, instead of Martha, and get closer to him without the distracting interactions of friends, family, and then corporate environment to report to.

I now know what it's like to live out the biblical verse (Genesis 50:20) where Joseph says, "What you meant for bad, God turned it around and used it for good." It turned out that through all the conflict with this boss, through being degraded, and then being asked to do tasks that even people who answered to my direct reports wouldn't do, God had a plan. I'm now living out Romans 8:28 where it says, "All things work together for the good of them who love the Lord and are called according to His purpose."

See, my boss gave those belittling tasks to me because he was trying to break my spirit and degrade me, but most of the pain I felt was in the physical, my feet. None of that could break me because I was built for adversity because God had fortified me with a mind-set and a work ethic that my Walmart boss said he'd never seen in his twenty years of executive leadership and that colonels in the army had recognized in me as a young captain. It's by God's grace I've soared through the good and the bad, having and maintaining only positive expectations through it all.

What I now know is that God had a plan. God wanted to move me out of there and into my "next" and to share with my spirit that that situation wasn't forever and that he had so much greater planned for me. This role was not my source.

God has a way of continually reminding me that he is the source, and my corporate roles were just the assignment for that season of preparation for my "next."

What is meant by "next" is the next best step, or stretch assignment, for God's glory and my growth.

Through the chaos and turmoil at work coupled with the corporate politics, God made a way. God made sure that even though I was a veteran diagnosed with PTSD, I still was able to keep it in check and have a mental toughness that allowed me to be in a good place and handle everything well that was going on. It truly is through him that I move, live, and have my very being.

It's in him that I boast and walk in confidence even during times of low self-esteem, fear, and obscurity.

People see my confidence in him and assume I am arrogant, but it's not my responsibility to shrink myself to their liking, and neither is it yours. Go forward, stay in momentum and always be greater than you were before.

Reckless abandonment is about breaking free from bondage to live a greater, more purposeful, God-centered life. Ideally, it's a time when you live your best life. BREAK FREE and live the best, blessed life with freedom to serve.

"You were running the race so well. Who has held you back from following the truth? It certainly isn't God, for he is the one who called you to *freedom*. For you have been called to live in *freedom*, my brothers and sisters. But don't use your *freedom* to satisfy your sinful nature. Instead, use your *freedom* to serve one another in love."

~Galatians 5:7-8, 13 NLT

SECTION 2

MARRY PURPOSE

"...Forget about what's happened; don't keep going over old history. Be alert, be present. I'm about to do something brand-new. It's bursting out! Don't you see it?

There it is! I'm making a road through the desert, rivers in the badlands. Wild animals will say 'Thank you!' —the coyotes and the buzzards— Because I provided water in the desert, rivers through the sun-baked earth, Drinking water for the people I chose, the people I made especially for myself, a people custom-made to praise me.

~Isaiah 43:16-22, MSG

CHAPTER 9

The Holy Spirit Is Key

"God has called us to live holy lives, not impure lives. Therefore, anyone who refuses to live by these rules is not disobeying human teaching but is rejecting God, who gives his Holy Spirit to you."

~1 Thessalonians 4:7-8, NLT

The Great Surrender

Transformation begins at the height of the decision to surrender. It can't happen when you're thinking about it. It happens when you have made up your mind that you will surrender.

Once surrender manifests, you will achieve a new level of maturity and a greater personal capacity. Surrender to what? I'm glad you asked. Surrender to changing, being better, developing more, perfecting your gift, and so much more. Most important, though, it means to surrender your will and your ways for his. Who's he? What's his name? Jesus. He's a consuming fire. He consumes our thoughts, minds, emotions, with His undying love and will enabling us to live a *free* life, if we let him. The grind or battle belongs to him and is not ours to toil or fight. In him, we experience a life *free* of sin, condemnation, shame, and judgment. It's a life where we walk in our wholeness and as a result, we reach back and pull others from their pits of hell! We're not the savior, so we point others to Him.

Apart from Him we can do nothing, but in Him we can do all things," according to Philippians 4:13: "I can do all things through Christ who *strength*ens me", my favorite scripture. We worship him with our testimony of his goodness, our acts of kindness, our yielding to his way. We worship him for whom he is, and we praise him for what he has already done. We don't manipulatively worship him for material acquisition, influence, or to have impact, but we receive them as by-products of his favor, also known as grace. Worship is all about spiritual sensitivity. It's an experience believer encounter when they hunger and thirst for more of him. Worship is impossible to fabricate because it's a lifestyle and not just a moment.

There are many phases of suffering and *obedience* God requires before there's a real manifestation. In Mathew 11:29 Jesus says: "Take my yoke upon you, and learn of me; for I am meek and lowly in heart: and ye shall find rest unto your souls. For my yoke is easy, and my burden is light." but then Paul declares differently to warn of the long suffering that comes with the great surrender in Philippians 3:10: "That I may know him, and the power of his resurrection, and the fellowship of his sufferings, being made conformable unto his death," People say the Bible has many contradictions, but it's important to know who's speaking and in which context the verses are being used. Furthermore, I'd like to think of those contradictions as seasons. In Ecclesiastes 3 the Bible declares, "There is a season for all things." We know there are reasons even when we don't always understand them. There's always another season of purpose or opportunity, meaning change is possible or that it may be coming.

When I think back over my life, I realize that I've made several pertinent transitions. Sometimes, it seemed like I was going backward, but in actuality, knowing what I know now, they were a pivotal part of my launching forward, very similar to a bow and arrow. To be jobless for a season seems backward.

Between my military service and my first job in the corporate sector, I didn't have a job for six months. I didn't have a plan when I recklessly abandoned the military, so to speak; I was in Iraq with ninety-five days of leave before I decided to ETS, or early terminate. At the time, I felt it was the best thing to do, and I don't regret that decision. I didn't expect to experience six months of unemployment, but it was necessary for me to draw closer to God. It was in that season that he gave me the divine instruction and growth I needed for my next assignment, the civilian career season. It was in that six-month "intermission," in 2004, that I received the gift of being able to speak in tongues according to Acts 2:4: "All of them were filled with the Holy Spirit and began to speak in other tongues as the Spirit enabled them." while praying in the privacy of my home. It was in that season I became an intercessor and experienced the manifestation of prophecy. Those were all an integral part of my foundational footing as a Christian.

It was in those times that I learned how to hear from God.

When you sow a lifestyle of worship, you receive divinely inspired downloads that only heaven can manifest.

People often tell me "they see my glory but they don't know my story." I'll say it how I feel it, "They see God's glory, but they'll never understand the process he took me through for the manifestation." One thing is true: He reigns on the just as well as the unjust, so these manifestations won't occur by work alone or else everyone would be justified in their boasting.

I now have the opportunity and time to experience God on a higher level. Isaiah 55:8 says, "His thoughts and His ways are so much greater than ours." God is all-knowing, and while we often don't understand, as we trust and obey, he begins to show us in little ways what he has in store for us. He's always concerned about every detail of our lives. We know He is with us even as we walk in new territory and greater dimensions. You see, God is building faith in you. He's growing you. He's moving you from where you are to a place of spiritual maturity that you may have never known before, and he is giving you extraordinary insight and wisdom so you can understand God's timing. Your new revelation allows you to experience supernatural and abundant peace. You will begin to do things his way instead of doing things your way and in His timing instead of yours. All of your life has been preparing you for such a time as this and are working together for His good in an effective, purposeful and Kingdom focused way.

Knowledge of the Word Activates the Holy Spirit

We can either feed our Holy Spirit or we can feed our fleshly desires the instant gratification they crave. Whichever we feed is what will grow and overpower our lives. When we read the word and apply it, we experience a more incredible life. The Holy Spirit is necessary for our *freedom*, which is also known as deliverance. This *freedom* is found throughout the word of God.

> "How can a young person live a clean life? By carefully reading the map of your Word. I'm single-minded in pursuit of you; don't let me miss the road signs you've posted. I've banked your promises in the vault of my heart so I won't sin myself bankrupt. Be blessed, GOD; train me in your ways of wise living. I'll transfer to my lips all the counsel that comes from your mouth; I delight far more in what you tell me about living than in gathering a pile of riches.

I ponder every morsel of wisdom from you, I attentively watch how you've done it. I relish everything you've told me of life, I won't forget a word of it."

~Psalm 119:9-16, MSG

We grieve and can cause the Holy Spirit to depart from us when we sin.

We must remember that *salvation* can be received in a moment of faith, but the *sanctification* process can take up to a lifetime depending on an individual's deliverance from various types of bondage. That's why some leaders, or pastors, can have an intellectual understanding of what needs to take place but lack the ability to stay *free* from the bondage of sin, the manifestation of true deliverance, in their lives. They allow the nature of sin, like any other believer, to overpower the Holy Spirit that is at work in keeping them *free*.

We're graced to move to the next phase without attaining full maturity in the previous phase, but we gain our greatest impact and influence once we reach levels of mastery in each phase. As a believer your greatest hindrance comes from never reaching a level of mastery, knowledge of the word, and being spoon-fed the word of God on Sundays. This spiritual malnutrition comes from you never really achieving your own revelation and level of understanding. This stagnation bleeds over into your social, professional, and even spiritual life with varying degrees of bondage. Your *freedom* is capped because you never reach a level of maturity, understanding, and wisdom. This *freedom* is synonymous with peace. This is the peace that guards our hearts and minds. Phillipians 4:7 KJV says, "And the peace of God, which passeth all understanding, shall keep your hearts and minds through Christ Jesus." This peace is ushered into our hearts by way of Holy Spirit. It's not enough to master knowledge of the word to the level of quoting and teaching it. While that's great leadership of others, full mastery is in great leadership to yourself. It's important for you to allow it to transform your private life beginning in your heart.

As mentioned earlier, people don't walk in true *freedom* and experience their best lives because their hearts are sick, and the only real physician is Jesus. When he operates on the heart, does the requisite heart surgery, there's a level of peace that comes upon you, his Holy Spirit. He keeps their hearts healed, pure, and whole. Hearts become contaminated when they grieve the Holy Spirit by the things they say.

"It's not what goes into your mouth that defiles you: you are defiled by the words that come out of your mouth."

~Matthew 15:11

"He receives Glory when we yield and allow His power, Holy Spirit, to purify our heart and our speech. Work through us. "Now all glory to God, who is able, through his mighty power at work within us, to accomplish infinitely more than we might ask or think."

~Ephesians 3:20, NLT

Deliverance

Transformation begins with deliverance.

Deliverance is really the process of breaking *free* from the sin (including dis*obedience* to God) that prevents you from walking in the necessary *freedom* you need to operate at your peak purpose capacity, which is assigned specifically to you by God. Deliverance requires a certain mind-set that's stronger than your personal desires. A weak mind is the ingredient for a defeated Christian walk. This is why it's imperative to consistently feed the mind so it becomes stronger than your self-will. No one is naturally self-righteous, so the mind has to constantly be fed righteousness, which is the word of God.

This is no different than needing to hear your favorite motivational speaker in the morning. The word of God should be so motivating and inspiring that it gets you pumped up to live right. I know you may be thinking things like, "but I don't understand it (the Bible); it puts me to sleep; it's difficult to concentrate on," yet others might think, "yes, it's so empowering." No matter where you are on your word walk, you can get to a place where you truly see it as life-altering.

What has helped me the most is prescribing to the bible app, You Version, which allows me to read thousands of amazing plans broken down by topic. It also allows me to compare double-digit versions of the same verse at once. It challenges me to be consistent and even to join in with my Bible-reading partners on various plans. It is the most engaging way I've found to read the word of God.

CHAPTER 10

The Process of Spiritual Maturity

"If it is to be it is up to me!"

William H. Johnsen

Before we can reach a level of spiritual maturity, God seemingly tests our *obedience* in phases. These phases are commonly referred to as "the process." People are always talking about "going through the process." This process is a journey toward spiritual maturity.

The Process of Spiritual Maturity

I'm circling back to make a point. In chapter 2, I briefly referenced Christians not demonstrating loving ways as a result of heart issues.

What most nonbelievers don't thoroughly understand is that Christian believers have a belief but not all have a deliverance.

They believed but they never reached maturity in the faith because they aborted the process when they subconsciously refused to fight for righteousness, absent of their breastplate of righteousness. There's a full deliverance process, and until believers have fully walked it out, they'll never be true ambassadors for the Kingdom of God. Many haven't walked out their love among their siblings in Christ, so the world doesn't stand a chance to experience the love of God through them.

The Phases of *Obedience*

If I may give my version of a Christian's faith walk and the process of spiritual maturity, which only comes through *obedience*, I would sum it up into the following four phases:

Phase 1: *Salvation*	The Belief and acceptance of Jesus Christ as savior ~ Romans 10:9-13
Phase 2: *Sanctification*	The process of transformation; purging from sin and separating for purity and seeking divine instructions to be used for God ~ Romans 12:2
Phase 3: Application	Applying Biblical principles to execute the vision of God ~ Matthew 6:10
Phase 4: Manifestation	To experience the results of your application ~ Ephesians 3:19-20; Romans 8:28

There are certainly more scripture references for each but the dominant scriptures are provided. Each phase is a prerequisite for the next. There won't be degrees of manifestation until there's commitment in each phase. When you mature in each phase, there will be greater levels of manifestation. It wasn't until Jonah's intention shifted that he was thrown from the belly of the whale and no longer bound. The same is true for our lives. God begins to manifest blessings on our down payment of intention until we fully commit and pay in full. However, we abort the full manifestation when we don't deliver on our promises.

Covenant is everything to God.

I'll briefly explain these monumental phases of *obedience* as a Christian.

Phase 1: The *Salvation* Phase

The *Salvation* Phase is the crawl phase of a Christian's walk, much like that of a newborn baby. It is the process of receiving Jesus Christ as your personal savior. It's the divine interruption from living your life randomly to making the decision to surrender to God for the purpose of being saved and accepting him as your personal savior. Many think they know this, but they really don't. In other words, it is the reason why Christ gave his only begotten son so that we may have the opportunity to live life more abundantly through *freedom* from sin while having the power to break curses, even if they are handed down through the generations, and to be set *free* from everything evil that comes to deteriorate our lives.

Salvation is just the beginning of a lifelong battle of spiritual testing, or warfare, most believers don't fully understand and aren't equipped for. *Salvation* is living in relationship with Christ daily and not just for a moment in time. It requires just as much of a relationship with God as it does with a person. This relationship with God is cultivated through fellowship in prayer, praise, and worship through the giving of time, talent, and money. For many, that's really basic knowledge but extremely difficult to consistently practice. Many times, people treat Abba Father, Jesus, the same way they do their natural father, mother, or relative, that is, not very well. If God requires us to honor our mother and father, how much more should we honor their creator? Honor demands more than a relationship; it requires sacrifice and intentional recognition.

Phase 2: The *Sanctification* Phase

The *Sanctification* Phase is the process of being purified in order to be a good fit for use by the Kingdom. During this process, God separates you so you can be perfected for his use. It's a lost season of your being away in a sort of wilderness, similar to military boot camp, so your spiritual mind can be conditioned while you learn his ways and his will for you. It's where you learn your kingdom gifts so you can be more effective.

Every time I'm in a season of isolation, I know now it's so God can purge, process, and promote me.

It's a season of consecration that requires keen, active listening and timely *obedience*.

The Bible tells us he's the potter and we're the clay, and he bends, breaks, and molds us for his use and his glory. *Sanctification* seems to be the most uncomfortable phase because it's usually overwhelming to be separated from people and activities that may have once dominated your life. It could require moving away or being abandoned by those you love because of your decision to change. Most important, it reprioritizes God as your number one priority while minimizing all other distractions.

The Struggle Is Real

In this phase, many fall off into sin because they don't have the power to live right and embrace God's will. For example, many single people have not mastered the ability to balance having God as their priority while in another personal relationship because of the many demands he imposes on them. I've certainly struggled in this area and absolutely believe it is one of the reasons he has allowed me to be in a state of singleness. I have to have the right person to complement me who will give me the space I need to include his plan for my life. This past year as I previously mentioned, I was even separated from my two closest friends due to their untimely deaths. Talk about heart wrenching. I hardly believe it was a part of my *sanctification* process because that would be too extreme a test from God, but it certainly served to isolate me forever from my greatest supporters and the people who en*couraged* me at all times.

During this *sanctification* season, there are necessary periods of consecration, to remove idols and distractors. It is a season of great purging to ready you for promotion to "next." Not everyone can accommodate the journey He has designed specifically for you. Ultimately, *sanctification* is the process of separating, purging, and preparing you so you can hear God more clearly to be empowered to execute in the Application Phase. The length of this phase is dependent on your consistency and intentionality.

Phase 3: The Application Phase

The third phase of *obedience* is the Application Phase. Now that you've separated, purged, and prepared through times of consecration, you are empowered to move forward in the things of God. Now you can move with certainty and clarity. This phase is all about execution in the space of many obstacles and hindrances.

Anytime it's a plan from God, there's great opposition.

These strong oppositions are demonically engaged spiritual warfare to stop the advancement of the Kingdom of God. A great example of this could be a person who was sent to prison so God could save his life. The person receives God in prison and becomes saved and even sanctified. The person will receive specific instructions while in prison. As soon as the individual is released, he is so excited to be *free* to do God's work but then is hit with all sorts of opposition. The person is now *free* so there are a lot more choices. The person could either push through and do what he said he was going to do while in covenant with God in prison, or he could follow his instinct for instant gratification and delay or deliver on the covenant he made with God.

Phase 4: The Manifestation Phase

This application is what generally releases the promises of God, also known as the fourth phase, called the Manifestation Phase. Manifestation comes to deliver what was promised and even more. Manifestation is when God's heart is so moved he opens doors no man can shut. He brings unparalleled favor and glory into your life to keep you en*couraged* along the journey especially as a new convert. He seems to really, really pour favor on new converts to allow them time to grow since they are accountable to their knowledge.

I've experienced this in my life and have witnessed it in many of the millennial Christians' lives I also follow. I'm Generation X and yes, humbled to say these millennials have been here before in their walk with Christ, laughing out loud. Being in covenant with God is the key to releasing the manifestation of "more" in your life, very similar to Quid Pro Quo.

Manifestation is receiving the promise or great reward for doing the hard work and graduating from the prerequisites of your divine God's purposeful assignment.

There are many phases of suffering and *obedience* God requires before there's a real manifestation. From Matthew 11:29, NLT:

"Take my yoke upon you. Let me teach you because I am humble and gentle at heart, and you will find rest for your souls. For my yoke is easy to bear, and the burden I give you is light."

Many people can't understand why the called are graced to do what they do. They don't obey because the way has been made easy for them; in fact, the responsibility they are called to bear is often weighty and burdensome. He also says to "get to know Him in the fellowship of His suffering," which is actually the fruit of the spirit. So when you have the Holy Spirit on the inside, in operation, it empowers you to "endure hardness as a good soldier."

People say the Bible has many contradictions, but I think it's all about perspective. I'd like to think of those contradictions as more like the change of seasons discussed in Ecclesiastes 3.

CHAPTER 11

Executing in *Obedience*

"But Samuel replied: "Does the LORD delight in burnt offerings and sacrifices as much as in obeying the LORD? To obey is better than sacrifice, and to heed is better than the fat of rams." 1 Samuel 15:22

It's always easier to see other people's flaws and sins but not our own. One of the greatest and often unacknowledged ways so many people are bound is in *obedience* to God. Whether or not you are in a relationship with him, he gives directions through many different vehicles of communication. There was a time I heard him but because I understood I was under grace, I still decided to do things my own way. I didn't realize my dis*obedience* to God was still a sin I was battling with.

We can be "willing" all day long but at some point, it has to transition to sheer execution. That execution is the *obedience* factor. It is one thing to be strong and another to have *courage*.

Much of our disobedience is caused by discouragement and fear.

Yes, we have the *strength* to be obedient but lack the *courage*. *Strength* means you have the capacity, but *courage* means not only do you have the capacity but beyond that you will do it in the face of fear, rejection, and past failures.

The Bible says, "If ye be willing and obedient you will surely eat the good of the land" (Isaiah 1:19-20, paraphrased). The problem was, I was eating the good of the land even when I wasn't being obedient. I felt I was receiving his favor to such an extent that I nicknamed myself "Confidently Favored" on social media.

Favor wasn't about what I received but rather about my receiving it in spite of my sins and feelings of unworthiness.

People don't understand the true meaning of the word favor. It's not just about receiving the blessings of God but receiving them in spite of being unworthy. Knowing what I know now, I'd prefer he give that favor to someone else and require me to level up sooner and live righteously in every area of my character. Fortunately, he knew what it took to get my attention when I no longer received his blessings, and his timing was impeccable. I had to endure withdrawal pains from no longer receiving his favor because I had been spoiled rotten. It was all a part of the process to drive me and so many others like me back to worship. The Bible says we should let patience have her perfect work in us.

We must be patient in the process of purposefully producing with perfection.

Then we will be afforded the opportunity to promote his promises.

Why are we so disobedient? We are disobedient because:

- We know God's grace and mercy is more than sufficient.
- We want to do things our way and be in control.
- We don't understand why God is telling us to do something.
- We fear the outcome of what God's telling us to do.
- We don't believe it's a good fit for our overall desires.
- We feel it's weird.
- It makes us uncomfortable.

The list goes on and on.

Have you ever considered the endless opportunities you could have if only you were obedient? Have you ever considered *obedience* as a form of worship? Have you ever considered all the benefits, rather than curses, you bring to your life when you obey God? If you served in the military, didn't you obey your commanding officers? How about in your church? In the corporate sector? Then why don't you obey God? Do you fear you're hearing him incorrectly? Are you concerned with failing in what he calls you to do? Is what he's asking you to do too inconvenient? Do you even recognize or hear his voice when he's speaking?

God speaks to each of us in many different ways. He speaks through people who are saved or unsaved. He speaks through dreams. He speaks through pastors. He speaks in the still, quiet times of meditation. He speaks while you're exercising and even on that long run. He speaks through a movie or television show. He speaks through your daydreams and visions. He speaks through his word. He speaks in worship. He speaks most clearly when you're fasting where he provides the greatest revelations. There are so many other ways he speaks to us. It's a matter of understanding what he's saying when he's speaking, and then it's our responsibility to pay attention. Finally, we must execute according to his instructions.

We are disobedient in one of two ways: Either we disobey the word of God or we disobey what he specifically tells us to do. Both of these ways are sins. The Bible says the wage of sin is death. There are some people who have sinned their way to death, and there are others who God graces longer for a reason only he knows. Not all sin leads to death but we are still chastened. The Bible says God chastens those he loves. In other words, he disciplines us when we don't obey.

There's nothing worse than being chastened by God. When that happens, you lose the favor of God. Where you were once blessed, you're then cursed. Life becomes harder. What you used to get easily, you begin to toil and work so much harder to receive. For example, you could lose a career or relationship that you used to once dominate or have under control.

There are countless examples of similar situations where the grace is no longer there. It's like your vertical relationship with the Father has been jeopardized by sin, and as a result, your horizontal relationships are impacted, and some of those relationships further negatively impact careers, businesses, and even happy homes. There are many scriptures to support this, but for the purpose of this book, you are simply challenged to go read the Old Testament and discover the many examples written therein. In summary, and as alluded to throughout the book of Deuteronomy, I've concluded these facts about what could be expected from operating in dis*obedience*:

- Dis*obedience* brings curses to our lives.
- Dis*obedience* renders us ineffective; we have low to no impact.
- Dis*obedience* causes us to miss opportunities.
- Dis*obedience* stagnates our growth.
- Dis*obedience* reveals our lack of wisdom.

Radical *Obedience*

I don't know about you, but I understand that our faith walk is a process that requires patience, sacrifice, and humbling.

It's not the type of process that can happen overnight because it requires a great level of learning, understanding, strategy, stewardship, and commitment that most people just aren't willing to endure.

It is only for the called, zealous, and trained at heart.

Once you break *free* from the sin and bondage that keeps you from hearing and understanding God's voice, the next step is to obey. Essentially, that's what the Application Phase is all about. Each person is different in his or her level of *obedience*, but most of the time the fruit, or manifestation, is indicative of the level of *obedience*. Timely *obedience* and delayed *obedience* yield different levels of fruit of course. So, it's imperative to understand seasons and timing.

It's also important to understand that trust plays a large factor in being obedient. That's why Proverbs 3:5-6 says: "lean not to your own understanding but in all your ways acknowledge Him because it's Him who will direct your path."

When people lean to their own analytical understanding instead of stretching their faith and obeying the voice of the Lord, not only do they close the door on manifestation, they also bring curses upon themselves.

I believe the level of understanding about curses drives some to be over-the-top obedient; these are the overachievers, the excellent ones. That fear of curses has humbled these people somewhere along the line. Ideally, this is what reckless abandonment is all about—realizing the critical timing and aggressively executing the will of God with careful *obedience*.

Again, the model prayer, discussed previously, suggests God's will and not our will. Yet, so many of us really don't live a life yielded to his will including many believers. We know when God is calling us to a higher calling, but we refuse because it makes us uncomfortable, and it requires us to walk in a greater level of stretched faith.

I remember a time when I brought curses of dis*obedience* on my business the moment I decided to make it an idol above what God was calling me to do.

I was seeking success in my business over significance in my purpose.

I didn't find his request to be convenient or appealing. I learned I was being selfish, and my selfishness adversely affected the spiritual progress of too many people whom I was assigned to be their spiritual mentor for a season. I had to repent and seek God for deliverance from these curses, and many of you will have to do the same thing.

Disobedience is caused by the lack of faith. We like to be in control and trust our abilities, but we can only do this for the planting of our faith. Our faith must be watered to grow, and unless God breathes favor on it, we are working in vain and will never see it increase.

The ability to consistently execute in radical *obedience* is a sure sign of spiritual maturity. By radical *obedience*, I mean reckless, without hesitation and over thinking. This is what separates the called from the chosen, the generals in the Kingdom, and the ones God makes rulers over the many, enlarging their territory because he can trust them. Increased *obedience* manifests in a mega way in the lives of those who have completely surrendered and recklessly abandoned their lives toward their greater purpose. It is a discipline we all struggle with, but a sure sign God rewards those who may fall but get back up, get it right, and soar higher. The increased manifestations experienced are not a sign of being unflawed but rather flawed and hyper-obedient, even if it requires people to recklessly abandon their current lives.

CHAPTER 12

Be Discipled

"For everything that was written in the past was written for our instruction, so that through endurance and the en*courage*ment of the Scriptures, we might have hope. Now may the God of endurance and en*courage*ment grant you harmony with one another in Christ Jesus, so that with one mind and one voice you may glorify the God and Father of our Lord Jesus Christ,"

Romans 15:5

If you have read this book and you really don't know the Lord Jesus Christ as your personal savior, you're challenged to know him in new and profound ways. He came so that you may have a more abundant life. No longer can Christians walk in defeat when Christ defeated death and rose with all power and left us with access to that same power. It is not about a particular denomination or religion because those traditions are man-made. It is all about our desire to be in fellowship and relationship with Christ Jesus and experiencing him in new ways as a result.

It's in intimate worship with Jesus Christ that we receive our greatest revelation and those God ideas. It's in this relationship you yearn to level-up, man-up, woman-up, and soar to heights unimaginable. Allow Holy Spirit to disciple you. When Holy Spirit is in full operation in you He teaches you and provides you great wisdom and revelation. God has a divine plan for your life and you will gain greater clarity of His plan the more you allow Holy Spirit to disciple you.

Among Other Believers

Your identity and purpose becomes clear in atmospheres of surrender and worship. If you're not in a good Bible-based church that operates in the fivefold ministry, pray and ask God to show you where to go. You will know it by the fruit of the people. They are walking in full deliverance. It is God's will for you to be in right fellowship with other strong believers of the faith.

There's nothing worse than being in a good church, in theory, but not growing spiritually. There should be strong, meaningful teaching because that revelation is what you need to empower your loins with the truth necessary to fight for your *freedom*, as previously mentioned.

Do not be in a rush to join. Wait for a confirmation from God. Take your time in selecting one as you would in selecting a spouse. It takes time to see certain dysfunctions, but there isn't a perfect church out there. You should partner with Holy Spirit on what your non-negotiables should be when it comes to selecting the right church. Viewing churches on social media is only half of the observation process. You have to visit the church to discern the atmosphere and understand the behind the scenes, the people you will be serving with. It's important to understand, over time and spiritual maturity, the heart issues imposed by those in leadership and how they might adversely impact you. Forewarned is forearmed.

To further explain what I mean, I experienced greater levels of pride and fornication, serving under leaders who struggled and never conquered their demons; but I didn't know better. I didn't realize it until I matured in greater understanding after leaving those situations. I experienced mean, back-biting, gossipy ladies and wondered why the spirit of anger crept into my life. I didn't know. There's no excuse. We're accountable for our own actions; we shouldn't shift blame onto others, but it's a lot easier to not have to be at war with spiritual demons your spiritual parents (church leaders) haven't conquered. There's a greater level of peace and *freedom* when you no longer have to deal with these dysfunctions. It's important to be led by those who are pure and victorious in the areas you are struggling in. No leader is perfect, so understanding where they struggle, through praying and interceding for them, and how their struggles may be impacting your heart is key to your personal *freedom* and growth.

Next Steps

You have a gift and if you are not in a church where the fivefold ministry is in operation, your gift may not be cultivated appropriately. This cultivation occurs when you are taught properly, you gain greater insight by using it, and then you grow in it. Your gift could be in operation outside of the church but you are admonished to bring your gift into the church house. There may be many members but the laborers are usually few. You make up the body of Christ so if every member is like you does that church ministry stand to thrive or barely survive?

THANK YOU!

Thanks so much for purchasing and reading this book!

As my gift to you for purchasing this book, please submit your information to receive a *free* download of the companion white paper by visiting ReadRecklessAbandonment.com. This white paper could be used for your individual or small group study.

I pray you received greater insight and feel empowered to soar higher in *freedom* and purpose. I certainly welcome your feedback since this is my first book. You can send it to readrecklessabandonment@gmail.com. *Contacting me on social media is my least preferred way of communicating with so much spam in my inboxes. It is my desire to provide you with a timely response.*

If this book inspired, empowered, and blessed you, and you would like to help me spread this message, please sow by leaving a review of endorsement on Amazon right now before you get busy and forget.

35852646R00084

Made in the USA
Middletown, DE
14 February 2019